concrete // rust // marrow

poems by

Connor Beeman

Finishing Line Press
Georgetown, Kentucky

concrete // rust // marrow

*To the queer people who were here before me, thank you.
And to my family and friends, who always believed
I had a book in me.*

Copyright © 2023 by Connor Beeman
ISBN 979-8-88838-164-9 First Edition
All rights reserved under International and Pan-American Copyright Conventions. No part of this book may be reproduced in any manner whatsoever without written permission from the publisher, except in the case of brief quotations embodied in critical articles and reviews.

ACKNOWLEDGMENTS

Thank you to the folks at the Lansing Poetry Club and the Ritzenhein Award for their kindness, support, and vital community work. Extra thanks to Alan Harris and Rosalie Petrouske for serving as mentors, and to Ruelaine Stokes for serving as an unofficial one. Grateful acknowledgement to these publications in which the following poems previously appeared:

Ghost City Review: "Art and Politics in the 1980s // Akron Art Museum"
New Reader Magazine: "today," & "river // DuPont // excess"
Black Fox Literary Magazine: "concrete // rust // marrow"
Oakland Arts Review: "I should have done something then, before the lake was choked"

Publisher: Leah Huete de Maines
Editor: Christen Kincaid
Cover Art: Abbot Handerson Thayer
Author Photo: Cody Phillips
Cover Design: Elizabeth Maines McCleavy

Order online: www.finishinglinepress.com
also available on amazon.com

Author inquiries and mail orders:
Finishing Line Press
PO Box 1626
Georgetown, Kentucky 40324
USA

Table of Contents

and I, too, am of this wreckage 1

today, ... 2

old match factory, east of town 4

for the second night, my thoughts linger on the façade 5

crooked river 6

river // DuPont // excess 7

I give you this, something unsaid 9

I should have done something then, before the lake
    was choked 10

in the parking lot of a long dead department store, ... 12

steel mill men 13

drugs into bodies // drugs into bodies 14

postcard litany 18

Erickson Power Station // Eaton County 19

it was here first 20

Art and Politics in the 1980s // Akron Art Museum 21

The Ashes Action 23

wounded concrete 25

on Highway 33, I tell you I feel ill 27

in the basement of my mother's house, there's a shelf
    of puzzles 29

Thursday, or the third day of rain in a row 31

concrete // rust // marrow 33

July 4th, the evening 34

and I, too, am of this wreckage

there is something dark and oily leaking
from the empty theater maquette.

the faded fireworks sign has streaks.
it wears wear and tear. it pulls itself apart.

the hospital closed last month, &
now I don't know who is left to do the healing.

there is the fear of God here.

  all around, in the dirt too,
    gritty and rough like stone.

but mostly above eye level,
  plastered like warning,
    a billboard promising absolution in a dirty field.

salvation is a promise no one is left to keep.

give me this wreckage,
and I will assemble what I can.

a twisted skyscape,
  a precarious thing,
    groaning in the wind.

it is dirty wire bent and woven,
    built into lattice, a monument, a web.

love, there is blood and rust
under my nails.

they are nearly the same color—
the same burnt-out red brown.

this place wants something from me.
I don't know what.

but I will make something of this.
there must be something in all of this.

today,

I fell into myself again.

I blame the gray-coated sky, the steel girder clouds,
  or the way this city gets under my skin in the little ways,
    like water in the cracks of a street freezing to wreak havoc on asphalt.

I am trying to be better, to be fairer,
but I did it anyways—gave over to that smog-cloud mind,
to that nothing-quite-right body.

in a bid to feel right, I struck out on my own,
and found myself in a dusty shop looking over old postcards,
  found myself searching my city once more.

love, how is it that the places we know best
can sometimes make themselves unrecognizable?

because there it is—that same water—bluer than I've ever known,
and the same buildings, always the same towers,

glancing up at me—unimpressed by my interest—
from fading cardstock in the back of the stacks.

I had to dig for my city,
  had to get my hands dirty to find my home,
    but what I find is so different from what I know.

one yellowed card, ink green,
calls Akron 'the city of opportunity.'

it paints downtown in bright, hope-stained colors.
trees everywhere, green, the buildings white and gleaming.

another shows the Cuyahoga carving its gorge, and
the then-new High-Level Bridge, all arches and concrete and pride.

I think of a mentor, far away now,
  who told me that our city's name meant 'high place' in Greek,
    that we were meant to be a city on the hill.

high place. crooked river.
a city nestled in the crest of a broken jaw,
unaware of how fickle opportunity could be.

sometimes, it feels like this past can't be true,
that some part of it must have been an illusion,
　but here we are—living in its remains.

I know that building, that bridge, that street.
　they are dirtier now. they do not gleam.

I think of what that mentor said last fall,
reading poems like these.

'name it,' he'd said then,
'don't be afraid to name this place.'

old match factory, east of town

you,
symbol.

you,
decay.

make yourself the meaning in all of this.

make your ivy unfurl.
weed your cavernous interior.

reclaim your smokestacks,
your industrial statements.

you once made fire itself,
can you do it again?

unsmash your windows,
  restore your tall glass eyes,
    make them look outward once more.

wear pride and vanity,
  make it ugly and uncompromising
    like coal ash and smoke.

return to what you were,
  just for a moment,

so that I can understand
  what you've become.

    what you intend to be.

for the second night, my thoughts linger on the façade

I don't know why I expect
answers from you.

maybe I am just hoping for
an explanation.

maybe I am looking for a reason—
  peering through your smashed-pane glass,
    as if answers hide on a dirty, empty floor.

there is not a time I have known you as intended.

I only know you in rust,
  in danger, or the closest
    thing this place can lay claim to.

I only know you in façade,
  as decay, brown brick
    cracking, history crumbling.

you are not called by your name.

you are called shame, loss, legacy—
  if you are spoken of at all.

when I watched the news with my parents as a child,
  it seemed that everything was ending.

overnight, a label smeared
Made in America became a weapon,
  became strife.

you were a first.
you were a siren.
  a warning.

if you had been heeded,
would that have mattered?

crooked river

this is my river.

it flows with water, with flood,
  with acid and metal and tar.

I have never swum in it.
  this has never been an option, never a choice.

you must understand—my river can burn,
  can spew ugly, blackish smoke like revenge.

flames have danced across it—made their home
in oil slicks and polluted film.

in a way, this is holy—
  the sight of water defying what water should be.

but it is horror too,
in another way.

it is the realization that our self-destruction runs deep,
  that it is in our water too.

its name, stolen centuries ago, means "crooked river,"
  named for the way it breaks its back against my city.

it carves through land older than all of us—
tracing a shape like the jaw of a bear,
  like the muzzle of a sallow wolf—nothing to lose.

a jaw, broken once, then again—heals unevenly.
  it will always be marred.

at its heart, between two rust-streaked cities, it threads itself
  through a national park—natural excess between steel-toed abuse.

even there,
it must remember what has been done.

there is nothing that water forgets.

river // DuPont // excess

I am crossing the river,
   the only river that matters—

the one that means border,
   that means distance.

the one that can only be bridged
with aching resolute steel.

I am driving myself across it.

   this is a new habit,
     an uncomfortable skin,

and I risk only a few glances
down towards the murk,
   that mighty rolling thing.

it is the same as it has always been.

brown and steady, powerful
in its own silent, unnoticed way.

night is falling—
   so the river eats the sun.
     it bleeds it out.

   orange, green,
     slick tan smeared with silt.

it allows the barges,
   the coal and the chemicals,
upstream only reluctantly,

like there's a grudge to be held
for all that's been done.

there is a factory,
all sprawl and steam.

it's DuPont,
on a street that bears the same name,
a highway exit dedicated only to its cause.

I have never known what
  they make there, not truly,
    only that it is somehow necessary.

that everything is somehow worthy.

but I do know that I boil
my water sometimes—
  just to be safe.

and I do know that the river is trying
to tell me something—

that this water's silence is no accident,

but I drive on.

as always,
I drive on.

I give you this, something unsaid

I grant you this place
  in all its legacy, in all its mirrors.

try not to break it,
  though you would not be the first.

my mother tells me that
  everyone ends up back here,
    whether they want to or not,

    that this place has a pull
      like a magnet, like a leech.

try not to believe her.

instead, take in the parks.
  the pond, drained and refilled once,
    the geese over swans.

take in the school that was mine.
  two low stories of red-brown brick,
    looming and obelisk and disk.

lose yourself in the used bookstore downtown,
  my favored labyrinth, our Echoes—the kind old women at the desk
    forever willing to give away a part of themselves.

it is older than anything here,
  except for all the things unspoken.

if you are willing, if you can trust
  that tug in your gut, then
    find me there.

kiss me there,
where no one will look.

betray no nerves.
betray nothing and no one at all.

there is no space for hesitation here.

I should have done something then, before the lake was choked

dive in.

the water is cool and crisp,
dark stone and chemical brine.

each summer the algae blooms,
  green and sticky and wrong,
    the lake brimming with rotting fruit,
      like a sheen of crabapples bobbing in the waves.

        it's worse each year.
            they say it's the pollution.

dive in anyways.

this is our lake.
  our water,
    no matter what it hides.

maybe there was a time to save it.
maybe there still is.

    but I'm not sure there's time to
    save anything anymore.

maybe all things are past the time for saving.

but do you remember being young?
  not knowing the words,
    but taking me past that scraggy tree line anyways.

past the buttress of the docks,
  the fort of that island,
    to that tiny stone beach,
      our private place,

      shattered beer bottles,
          glass glinting like warning.

do you still remember that sunset?

how orange the sky was
  that it stained the lake in its hues,
    red and orange like rust and blood.

I wanted to kiss you then.
I was twelve and I already knew that was wrong.

    I wanted it anyway.

I remember watching a water snake, now endangered,
cut confidently through the waves.

I never liked them, I'd surrender the lake when I saw one,
  but you didn't care, never showed fear like that.

nothing in that lake could scare you.
sometimes, I wonder if that's still true.

in the parking lot of a long-dead department store,

I reach for you across the center console,
cautious at first and then caution-less.

I do not know what I am doing, not yet,
and neither do you.

this is the way of things when you
are still too young to know better.

we want only to be wanted. we stake no claim to love.
the words would feel too large, too unfamiliar on our mouths—

> their inaccuracy like crooked teeth,
> like oversized pills refusing to fall
>   down our throats.

back then, a part of me thought
I could claim nothing—not even what I could touch.

so when I meet you in the shadow of the empty store—

> I am nothing but what you tell me to become.
> you are everything you were told not to be.

we are easy-rough, tender-foolish,
drunk on a conditional trust.

we do not know it yet, but across the lot is a movie theater
a pandemic four years out will kill—the last one in town.

even there, beneath neon lights perpetually unglowing,
we couldn't imagine there was more to lose.

the next day, I will meet a friend
at the Goodwill next door.

she will run her hand over discounted fabrics,
  once and twice owned. I will laugh and buy
    clothes that don't fit on purpose.

when we walk out into the parking lot,
I will do my best not to think of you.

instead, I think of how different
this scene looks in the sun.

steel mill men

I have seen men shatter themselves.
they do it all the time.

hand them wreckage,
  rusted steel, rebar all jagged,

and ask them to name it, to make something of it.

across a skyline of smokeless smokestacks,
watch them drive it through their ribs instead.

watch them bleed rust-red, overdose
on medicines with unpronounceable names.

like us all, they are mourning the past—
  the steel mill men.

the union men, the bricklayers, the blue-collar grit.
  all masculine, all industrial—the line between the two dissolving—
    as uneven and rough as auto-line hands.

but the factory's been closed for decades,
  so the men I know now lay themselves bare on unused train tracks.
    they pull at their scabs in overgrown parking lots.

compare them to the man on the factory line—
  the Spartan in a steel mill—
    and watch men turn themselves to air.

how do you become a man when what makes a man is gone?
what can a queer boy grow up to be when this is all he sees?

the men of my grandfather's generation are gone now.

all that is left is murals that remake them as myths,
  splaying men with hard hats and soot on stone-set jaws
    across the battered walls of my town.

all that is left is the legacy.

and we are still here—still staring up at their likeness,
  still asking them how to be.

drugs into bodies // drugs into bodies

I.

I have seen dead men
in my hometown paper.

some days, it feels as if the pages swell with their faces,
obituaries with careful wording.

here, addiction is not mentioned
until it demands our attention,
and every death is an unforeseen tragedy.

the word overdose is a hushed kind of speech—
tragic gossip at the supermarket, on the sidewalk.
it lives and dies in that quiet.

there is a shame here. it runs deep.
it's in the iron, in our blood.

but I know now that shame is a tool that must
be worn down, that silence can be death,

for my elders have taught me these things
in a different century, in a different life.

they taught me how life can feel like death,
how blood can taste like rust.

II.

I have seen dead men in the BAR
I find them while chasing the past.

a new disease, a purple cancer becomes GRID becomes AIDS,
becomes 10,000 dead by '86 and no one has answers.

I am angry, as always, that generation-old tightening in my throat,
 that rage without words that demands them anyways.

but after enough pages, enough weeks of
an obituary section heaving like fluid-filled lungs,
  all I can be is empty.

hollow loss. desolation as legacy.
a generation gone and I can't possibly learn all their names.

so instead, I try to remember
all their faces.

III.

I have a friend from high school who's dead now.
I have forgotten the sound of his voice, have almost forgotten his face.

another's brother is gone too, tragedy once removed.
  another's in treatment, last I heard, but I don't ask much.
    there is always a reason to look away.

I think of a family friend, a paramedic, a rust-worn man,
  who still flinches each time he gives Naloxone,
    the new drug designed to save us from medicine.

he says it's like they rise from the dead—
like they're reborn in fury, back from hell itself.

their pulses erratic,
  as if to prove they still have one.

the first sound back—something unholy
and sacred, something desperate and gritty.

but they are alive.
despite it, they are alive.

IV:

in 1988, queer people like me fell
to the ground on the steps of the FDA.

they recreated what they saw all around them—tried on death's silks—
so that those with power would see what happened without their treatments,
    without the medicines they held behind publicly funded doors.

'drugs into bodies,' we chanted then,

and laid out our demands on hand-painted canvas,
laid our bodies rag-limp for all to see.

insistent, angry in the power,
powerful in their anguish—

they made themselves known in the way only those
who had already lost everything could.

for once,
the world couldn't look away.

so when they were dragged away by bullet-faced police,
   shouting even then, fighting even then,

they had got what they needed,
   or at least the start of it.

drugs into bodies.
drugs into bodies.

V:

the police in my town, cop-callous,
say they're tired of giving Naloxone to the same addicts.

as if life is something to grow impatient with, a cost to be cut,
as if some people—coping jaggedly—have earned their pain.

I tell my younger brother to be careful who he buys his weed from,
   to be careful what he tries, to tell his friends to be careful too.

still college-reckless at heart, I am the last to judge,
but truthfully, I am scared.

I am scared of another obituary with a name I recognize,
  scared of our inversion of medicine.

there is already so much gone here,
and now the people hollow themselves out too.

thirty years ago, people like me demanded treatment, demanded to live.
now, the people I grew up with find new medicines to die with.

and I don't know how to save them.
I don't know how to speak to all that's lost.

postcard litany

one card from the turn of the good century,
one from the turn of another.

one card all blue skies added in post,
another gray-overcast and honest.

one card viaduct of old—civic arches and metro pride
and concrete catching light in a way it no longer can.

another the low sitting Y-Bridge across the same gorge,
the bridge we took to see a grandfather in the hospital.

one card muddy falls—nature's reckoning—
another the park we've tucked between our excess.

one card The Flats in motion, another The Flats static—
in both the river is re-colored far too blue.

one card signed from a man long dead to a wife long gone,
asking her to join him soon in 'the city of opportunity.'

one card Cleveland's skyline, the lake angry behind it.
  towers and water the same grays, painted from the same palate,
    as if they are waiting to see which will outlast the other.

one card the river twisting like a snake's dying throes,
  the same card the city watching.

Erickson Power Station // Eaton County

a few miles away, a coal ash pond spills into water wells,
and no one knows anything until everyone must know.

there it is again—our poison slick, cruel, and self-inflicted.

everywhere I've lived, I've felt it, heavy
in all the wrong ways like lead from the tap.

sometimes, it feels as inescapable
as this place—tar-sticky, webbed memory.

I think of all the water I've boiled—
of all the pots set out on high,

of taking my grandparents to a restaurant &
a waiter replacing our glasses with plastic bottles mid-meal.

'boil order,' the words on his lips, apologetic.
boil order water sitting heavy in my stomach.

I think of air quality warnings sent to my phone all summer long—
of haze over the mountains, smoke from fires out west even here.

the tightness in my lungs—the air not quite right, not quite air anymore—
the way the sky itself reminds us of our bodies' limits, of our fragile frames.

I think of the microplastics that must sit in my gut now,
in my bones, in the bodies of everyone I know,

in the same way they must make a home in the ocean,
in the innards of creatures who have no part in this.

lithium, boron, 'dangerous contaminants.'

our river we do not fish from, that we do not swim in,
that scoured itself to the bone so we would see what we'd done.

the land and ocean and river and lake all bruised,
all pity and rage and reflection and stare.

they are asking what we'll submit to—
if we'll agree to drink the water we have.

it was here first

I swam in the Ohio only once.

I was a child then, half-floating in deep murk,
    clinging light to the ladder of a boat
        that we did not own.

head back in the water,
    hair wet like dew,
        a polluted baptism.

all there was to notice was the pull,
   the tug of that insistent water.

the river had somewhere to be.

     a vendetta.
     a cause.
      a desire

for that silt-ridden collision
with the Mississippi three states away,
    for tan water folding into brown.

I wondered what would happen if I let it have its way,
    let it pull me from this place,

tumbling like driftwood,
    like the waterlogged weeds
        and the mining runoff.

it was so quiet then,
   in that moment,
      in that vastness between conceded banks.

the river, just that once,
was empty.

it was its own
and I was nothing.

it was the way things were meant to be.

Art and Politics in the 1980s // Akron Art Museum

north of the city's heart, I wander
the art museum's chest with you.

it's a Tuesday, the building nearly empty,
and there is a visiting exhibit on AIDS.

it takes me by surprise, around the corner,
all my strength undone by withered bodies and protest signs.

there is nothing to say, just your hand to reach for,
as the quiet videos play on loop for a silent gallery.

sometimes, I wonder what it could have meant to know one of these men,
to know them full-bodied and foolish—unaware of any virus.

would they have taught me how to live?

would they grant me the wisdom of a queer elder—
the ever-vital knowledge of survival? the ever-elusive promise of our joy?

could they have told me what belonging would feel like when I needed it most?

told me that one day I would feel it heavy in my gut,
light in my chest, in my very bones and radiant through my fingers
  as I danced in a crowded club—just as they had.

maybe, but there is
no way to know.

what's done is done.
what's lost is lost.

sometimes, I want to feel fractured,
  as if I've earned the shattering.

four highway lanes, all empty,
off a cloverleaf interchange.

an IV plunged deep, medicine's expressway to the veins,
carrying saline and antibiotics and never enough time.

sometimes, I want to bleed for my city, weep for my elders,
but I see them as separate wards, separate bodies.

more often, we are one and the same.

some of us came home from the coasts to die.
　some of us never made it back.

some of us never left, did everything right,
　and our bodies failed us anyways.

I am always relearning the nature of crossroads,
reminding myself to consider it all.

on the screen, a dying man in a nursing home I know
　says his name for the camera.

in this quiet white, it is the only sound
　I can hear.

The Ashes Action

On October 11th, 1992, ACT-UP staged 'The Ashes Action,' where protestors marched to the White House carrying the ashes of loved ones they'd lost to AIDS. Outflanking the police, many successfully dumped their ashes onto the White House lawn in an angry and resonant protest of the Bush Administration's continued failure to adequately address the AIDS Crisis.

It is a Sunday.

it is a Sunday in 1992 and you march

to the beat of a solemn, uneven drum
down Pennsylvania Avenue.

you are flanked by cops.
they watch you warily.

you are flanked by grief.
  it has no words.

instead, you carry it in a hand-decorated box,
  a miniature urn,
    in a plastic tub that
      is all you can afford.

him, her, them—the one you lost,
the many you've lost, the one of many—
  are in that box.

you tell a reporter that this was your lover.

you tell a reporter you've lost so many that
fresh grief feels like morphine.

their names are a sea of loss,
  a churning, angry ocean of neglect.

but their body is politics—is power itself—now.

they have known,
  known longer than anyone else,
    that their bodies have always been politics.

to dump the ashes of your dead
    their charred skin,
  their chipped bone,

onto the lawns of their killers

takes a bravery
I cannot imagine.

it requires a pain
I cannot fathom.

to say their names into a megaphone is
hollow absolution.

how many eulogies can we stand?
how many names will fill an afternoon?

what can be done for your loss,
  for their failure,
    for our reality?

there are so many gone
and still—no answers.

there are so rarely consequences.

there are only
ashes on the lawn.

wounded concrete

I.

in the summer after the quietest spring,
  you asked why all our highways lead nowhere.

and I didn't know what to say then, how to answer
  your question because I didn't understand what you couldn't see.

love, the answer was all around us.

it was in the paint-chipped houses that sagged,
  weary, nearly comatose at the freeway's edge.

in the roads weather-marred,
  the part of town I take the long away around.

but the things that are obvious
must not always be, and I suppose

I cannot expect you to speak a language
  where all the words are unspoken.

fluency is no gift, no absolution,
but it is a tool, a hardy shield.

we make our homes in the body of the city,
  the hollowed-out chest,

  but we never admit it,
can never truly speak of what's been lost.

concrete can shatter,
but it can never be wounded.

II.

love, I want to tend to my city's wounds,
  make myself its haggard nurse,

    but the wounds have already healed uneven.
    the bones have set crooked—malunion.

I came too late to save anything,

but I came soon enough to wait at the bedside,
  to breathe in the staleness of a nursing home room,
    the acrid smell of the after.

do you remember it, love?

that moment two Novembers ago as you drove through Canton—
  the city raw, rusted rebar under a bone-gray sky.

the way I looked out the window then,
how couldn't tear myself away

from the billboard promising God
or the water stains that marred it.

you asked me what was wrong,
and I couldn't explain it to you.

it was a feeling without words—
a feeling in a language you couldn't understand.

on Highway 33, I tell you I feel ill

roadkill.

a rabbit facedown,
  streaked with its own blood,
    smear of brown-red self behind it like ash.

a deer this time, a few miles down,
  legs splayed in a final way,
    neck bent unmistakably.

there are flies. you are driving
  faster than you need too,
    but I can still see the flies.

love, I don't know how we can stand to
live in it anymore—the sheer violence of the world.

maybe you are rougher, thick-skinned like men should be,
but I have never been as strong as I was told to be.

sometimes I feel like I was made porcelain—
my grandmother's finest china locked away and undeployed—
  and then told to shatter.

it all feels so pointless,
so senseless, and I am tired
  of burying myself from the terror,
    the pain, the emptiness of it all.

    nothing has to die—
and if it must, why must it die like this?

what does a creature think before
its back is broken by steel?

entrails—the body undone—strewn on pavement,
  on the angry grass that clings to the highway's side.

when I tell a friend that I can't help but imagine how it happened,
  they snark, 'usually by a car.'

I cannot wear cruelty like others, love,
  or opt for blindness like you.

I don't know where you learned to avert your gaze,
  but I would like to sample the immunity.

in the basement of my mother's house, there's a shelf of puzzles untouched

world-weary,
I pour a puzzle onto the table.

this is a new ritual,
a way of reclaiming sense,

and as I sit there, dragged pieces apart,
matching colors and the hazy ghosts of shapes,

I think of my mother and her mother—
the one she does not speak to anymore.

I think of their silence,
both then and now.

I think of them years ago, sat over the table,
eyes intent and searching just like mine now—
   saying nothing, all their being to the task at hand.

their hands, one still young and one old even then,
reaching surely to place pieces exactly
   where they were meant to be.

when my grandparents came to visit,
   (only ever once a season)

my mother would pull out the same puzzles
from the basement shelf, and select one carefully—

   though it was almost always the wreath
   (the one her mother had given to her).

it was their ritual, one of their many ways
   to connect despite the months apart.

it was the same as the trips to the department store—
   the ones where they gossiped and bought nothing.

 or their meandering conversation while cooking,
   the way they anticipated each other's every move.

it was their connection, and I, boyish in name,
  knew I could never be a part of it.

  there were always more important things to do,
    a game to watch, a trail to cut through muddy woods.

    a club or bat or ball to be placed in my hand
      as if I would intrinsically understand its use,

      as if I, being who I was supposed to be,
  would always understand these things.

even then, even young,
  there were certain things I knew were not mine,
    certain things I knew not to want.

the feminine, no matter what it was,
  did not belong to me. it could not
  be wanted.

but I sit here now, glass of wine in hand,
  the puzzle's frame half-formed and curled like ivy,

and I think not of my mother and grandmother's silence,
but of what they must have talked about.

I think of what it could have meant
to have a seat at their table.

Thursday—or the third day of rain in a row

you say the ground smells here,
  as if that's a fair assessment.

that when it rains, which it always does,
  dreary and unromantic,

the earth itself stinks,
  adding insult to injury.

love, we are unfair to this place.
we both know it.

but still, we are callous.
we are letting blood to assuage our wounds.

I miss our adopted mountains.
I can tell you do too.

the ones that watched oceans be born,
the ones that were once taller than all the world's peaks,

but allowed themselves, graciously, to be made smooth,
  to be remade into something old and new
as the seas split between them.

they welcomed us, a child of rust and steel
and an evermoving perennial, without judgement.

they let us refashion ourselves where so many had before.
in the hills, among the trees, in a town that
staked its claim along a muddy stream.

I remember—hiking with you—
coming across a tall, stubborn boulder,
  moss-covered in the foothills.

we climbed it then, found handholds
in the cool stone and damp green,
till we reached the top.

even perched there, the hills surrounded us,
still higher, still holding us in their careful shell.

though not ours to begin with,
those mountains bent for us anyways.

they let us make our home between their rounded peaks,
along the bend of a shallow silt-stained river.

do you remember it love,
all the details of the final summer?

how in the mornings, we would wake to see
not just the sky, but the earth itself,
  rising to meet us.

concrete // rust // marrow

my town is tired.

it is rust and gold.

indigo match
   and burnt-out brick.

it is factories in amber,
   coal once long ago.

rubber and steel
   and burning water.

we built you once.
   we decay nonetheless.

my town is weary.

it is ribs,
   stray dog,
     marrow sucked dry.

it is resilience.
   weeds in cracks,
     unkillable and yellow-green.

it is persistence,
   stubborn land and stubborner concrete.

it is opioid, overdose,
   abuse.

it is legacy, history,
   endurance.

my town is an echo.
hear it.

decay, renewal.
ending, beginning.

July 4th, the evening

in the field next to us, the children chase fireflies.

they grab flying, flickering ember,
  and hold it in their hands.

with fire cupped in their palms—
  they are endless and don't even know it.

we watch from a balcony,
  perched upon rocks, off a borrowed apartment.

at our feet are the fruits of our labor,
  flowers in bloom and herbs in excess.

the air is acrid—the lingering smoke of fireworks lit early.

every few minutes, the sky erupts into flames.
   it is a kind of celebration.
      it is a careful thing, fire, being handled without care.

there is a star out already—a single jewel.

I tell you it is Venus, the evening star,
    but to be truthful I'm not sure,
       though I want it to be Venus.

sometimes, I feel like I know nothing
and everything all at once.

sometimes, I feel as if the world happens to us,
like we are the silt being dragged down our river.

this afternoon, we twisted in a pool till we couldn't any longer,
   your hands around my legs, my waist, and my own arms claiming
     ownership over you, wrapped around your chest.

we swam till we came undone,
    until we shed our skin, came out of the water
       as something entirely new, though we had no name for it.

that feeling. that tug in my gut.
the desire to know it all, to feel everything.

love,
I think I want to be endless.

I think I want to hold fire like children do,
in that reckless way, in that harmless way,

like they know nothing of the world
except that it is their own.

Connor Beeman (he/him or they/them) is the winner of the 2022 Ritzenhein Emerging Poet Award. He grew up just outside Akron, Ohio and attended Ohio University—where he received his Bachelor of Arts in Creative Writing, and Women's, Gender, and Sexuality Studies. As a queer writer, they have always worked to create and uplift work that celebrates the marginalized. Currently, they live in Lansing, Michigan, where they write and work as a librarian.

Their work focuses on themes of queerness, post-industrial space, and history. Previous publications include *Ghost City Review, New Reader Magazine,* and *Black Fox Literary Magazine.* This is his first chapbook.

www.ingramcontent.com/pod-product-compliance
Lightning Source LLC
Chambersburg PA
CBHW031818110426
42743CB00057B/988